FORD MUSTANG

Mike Mueller

First published in 1995 by MBI Publishing Company, PO Box 1, 729 Prospect Avenue, Osceola, WI 54020-0001 USA

The information in this book is true and complete to the best of our knowledge. All recommendations are made without any guarantee on the part of the author or Publisher, who also disclaim any liability incurred in connection with the use of this data or specific details.

We recognize that some words, model names and designations, for example, mentioned herein are the property of the trademark holder. We use them for identification purposes only. This is not an official publication.

MBI Publishing Company books are also available at discounts in bulk quantity for industrial or sales-promotional use. For details write to Special Sales Manager at Motorbooks International Wholesalers & Distributors, 729 Prospect Avenue, PO Box 1, Osceola, WI 54020-0001 USA.

Library of Congress Cataloging-in-Publication Data
Mueller, Mike.
   Ford Mustang/Mike Mueller.
   p. cm.
   Includes index.
   ISBN 0-87938-990-7
   1. Mustang automobile—History. I. Title.
   TL215.M8M84   1995
   629.222'2—dc20   94-48210

On the front cover: This beautiful 1966 Mustang Hi-Po 289 convertible is the pride and joy of Bill and Janien Bush, Champaign, Illinois.

On the frontispiece: As part of Ford's "It was, it is" revisionist theory for the '94 Mustang, the fully floating running horse logo was nicely incorporated into its grille much like those of its celebrated predecessors.

On the title page: This striking yellow 1971 Mustang Mach 1 belongs to Charlie and Pam Plylar, Kissimmee, Florida.

On the back cover: This 1994 Mustang SVT Cobra convertible was provided courtesy of Jim Sawyer and Dan Reid of Ford's Special Vehicle Team in Detroit.

Printed in China

Contents

Acknowledgments

Comparing the all-new '94 Mustang to its '64-1/2 ancestor on a beautiful fall day in Atlanta last year during one of the many Ford-sponsored celebrations of its latest ponycar rendition was only natural. As the ads proclaimed, "It was, it is." And with the photo appearing here, so began my quest to photograph as many Mustangs as possible for this short-winded epic. Hmmm, 30 years of Mustangs, where to begin?

Now that all that is done, the time comes to thank all the not-so-little people who made all my sweat possible. People like my brother, Dave Mueller, of Flat ville, Illinois, who never fails to come through for me when I'm on one of my many Midwest photo jaunts. Then there's sister Kathy Young, of Champaign, Illinois, my wife, Denise, and good friend Leslie Mathis, both here in Lakeland, Florida, all able-bodied Mustang pilots who each took turns behind ponycar wheels while I did all the snapping. And speaking of test drivers, I certainly can't forget little Teddy Mueller, who literally put the pedals to the metal in one of AMF's Midget Mustangs, owned by good sport Dale Richeson in Tuscola, Illinois.

Also from Tuscola, Mustang collectors and all-around great folks Tom and Ruthi O'Brien went well beyond the call of duty while allowing me access to their great cars. Of note as well is an equally great group of guys known as the Central Illinois Mustangers, Bernie Doty, Dennis Crow, Jim Fannin, Max Dilley and Dave Gass, to name just a few. Florida Mustangers Glenn Bornemann and Frank Cossota were of priceless assistance, too.

A big thanks also goes to Henry "Butch" Schroeder, of the Midwest Aviation Museum in Danville, Illinois, and his ace righthand man, Mike Vadeboncoeur, for letting me use Butch's fabulous F-6D P-51 Mustang fighter plane as a photo prop of all things. And I also can't thank noted Georgia musclecar collector Milton Robson and Wayne Allen enough, Wayne being Robson's highly talented restoration guru.

Other debts of gratitude are owed to Jim Sawyer and Dan Reid at Ford Special Vehicle Team in Detroit for the loan of not one but two '94 SVT Cobras. Tom Boyle, Anne Booker, and Barbara Kinnamon, Ford's public affairs people in Atlanta, also allowed the use of two '94 GTs. And an additional hot ride came courtesy of Dario Orlando of Steeda Autosports in Pompano Beach, Florida, who put me behind the wheel of his excellent '94 Steeda Mustang. Special thanks also go to Robert F. Tasca Sr. and his family, Robert Jr., Carl, David and Bobby III, in Rhode Island for their cooperation, patience and, above all, their hospitality.

Finally, this book could not have happened at all without the additional cooperation of the various feature car owners. Although I'd love to thank each one individually, space constraints permit only so much hot air in one blast, so one hearty thank you will have to do. In basic order of appearance, these people are:

Robert Deale III, Atlanta, Georgia, '64-1/2 289 convertible (red, this section); Max and Joyce Dilley, Urbana, Illinois, '67 GT coupe; Peter and Beverly Fagan, Urbana, Illinois, '67 GT fastback; Charlie and Pam Plylar, Kissimmee, Florida, '71 429 Cobra Jet Mach 1; Donald and Pam Farr, Mulberry, Florida, '66 GT coupe; Tom and Carol Podemski, South Bend, Indiana, '78 King Cobra; Mike and Denise Mueller, Mulberry, Florida, '88 GT convertible; Dale Richeson, Tuscola, Illinois, '64-1/2 260 coupe; Sam Munro, Dunedin, Florida, '64-1/2 289 convertible; Paul and Carolyn LiCalsi, Orlando, Florida, '65 289 2+2 fastback (red); David and Marilyn Gass, Rantoul, Illinois, '65 six-cylinder 2+2 fastback (blue); Bill and Janien Bush, Champaign, Illinois, '66 Hi-Po 289 convertible; Jim and Lynda Fannin, Bloomington, Illinois, '66 Hi-Po 289 GT coupe; Max and Joyce Dilley, Urbana, Illinois, '67 GTA convertible and '68 California Special; Tom and Ruthi O'Brien, Tuscola, Illinois, '68 fastback; Chris and Deborah Teeling, Enfield, Connecticut, '68-1/2 428 Cobra Jet fastback; Dennis and Kate. Crow, Oakwood, Illinois, '69 428 Cobra Jet Mach 1; Milton Robson, Oakwood, Georgia, '69 428 Super Cobra Jet convertible; Bernie and Zona Gail Doty, Strasburg, Illinois, '70 Boss 302; Barry Larkins, Daytona Beach, Florida, '70 Boss 429; Steve and Stacy Collins, Jacksonville, Florida, '71 Boss 351; Ralph Gissal, Land O Lakes, Florida, '72 Olympic Sprint convertible; Tom and Carol Podemski, South Bend, Indiana, '73 convertible, '75 Mach 1 and '84-1/2 20th Anniversary hatchback; Jack McAllister, Dallas, Pennsylvania, '79 Indy Pace Car replica; Tom and Ruthi

O'Brien, Tuscola, Illinois, '83 GT, '83 5.0 convertible and '66 Shelby GT 350; J.D. Anderson, Vero Beach, Florida, '86 SVO; Dave Geiger, Elkhart, Indiana, '65 SOHC A/FX factory dragster; Dave Robb, Titusville, Florida, '67 Shelby GT 500; Dennis and Kate Crow, Oakwood, Illinois, '69 Shelby GT 350; Bill and Janien Bush, Champaign, Illinois, '69 Shelby GT 500 convertible; Bill and Barbara Jacobsen, Odessa, Florida, '70 Shelby GT 500; J. R. and Rita Castle, Clearwater, Florida, '90 ASC/McLaren; Ken and Mary Jean Wesche, Mulberry, Florida, '87 Saleen.

Again, thanks so much, all.

In the beginning Ford's Mustang represented affordable, practical sportiness, but that didn't mean ponycar buyers couldn't dress their mounts to the nines. Among the wide array of convenience, performance and appearance options initially offered in 1965 and '66 was this attractive styled-steel wheel. Shown here is the 1965 version.

1 Introduction

Thirty Years Down The Road And Still Kicking

They came from far and wide across this country, as well as overseas, automotive enthusiasts by the tens of thousands—including one president of the United States—all headed for Charlotte, North Carolina. The date was April 17, 1994. The reason for the mass exodus? A birthday party, a 30th anniversary celebration honoring the car that has probably turned more heads—among them Bill Clinton's—in its time than anything ever to roll out of Detroit. Trends, fads, and

Left: A ponycar progression. Shelby American's first GT 350 Mustang variant (back) is shown with Ford's original Mustang and two of its "prototype" predecessors, the mid-engined, two-seat Mustang I racer (front) from 1962 and the Mustang II showcar (directly above the Mustang I) of 1963.

commander-in-chiefs have certainly come and gone over the last three decades, but Ford's Mustang has never left and remains running every bit as strong today as it did when it first hit the ground in a gallop in 1964. Thirty years on the job and still a winner—now that's something worth celebrating. Wonder if Mr. Bill took any notes?

Interestingly, Washington's Oval Office has been home to seven presidents since Lee Iacocca grabbed all the limelight immediately following the Mustang's official introduction on April 17, 1964. Kicking off a feeding frenzy the likes of which American automobile dealers had never seen before, Dearborn began rolling out those little affordable Mustangs with their long hoods, short rear decks, bucket seats, and floor shifters as fast as buyers could rope 'em in. Editors at *Time* and *Newsweek*

While many purists gasped, most among the automotive press were pleased with the Mustang's new body for 1967, a larger, more rounded shell created basically to make room for the breed's first big-block powerplant, the 390cid FE-series V8.

were so impressed with the "newest breed out of Detroit" they both immediately featured Iacocca and his hot-selling baby in prominent cover stories. Another high-profile honor quickly followed as the Mustang was chosen to pace the 48th running of the Indianapolis 500 in May 1964.

Twelve months later, Mustangs were still making news as production surpassed 417,000; that topped Detroit's existing record for first-year sales established in 1960 by Ford's Falcon. Yet another major milestone came in February 1966 when the millionth Mustang left the line. Hands down, no one has ever done it any better.

Of course Iacocca wasn't the only mover-and-shaker behind Dearborn's amazing mass-market marvel. Donald Frey, product planning manager; Hal Sperlich, his assistant; Donald Petersen, marketing man (later to become Ford's president); Gene Bordinat, styling chief; Joe Oros and Dave Ash, stylists; and many others promoted the roles in conception, design, promotion, and production of the Mustang. But it was up-and-coming Lee Iacocca as Ford vice president and division chief who stood ready, willing, and able to accept the lion's share of the credit.

Then again, only one man can be the father of anything, and if any one Ford man deserved that honor alone it had to be Iacocca, simply because the original idea of mass producing a small, affordable, youth-oriented automobile was his. And from there, it was his dedicated efforts to untie Henry Ford II's commonly knotted purse strings that singlehandedly transformed dreams into reality. As Donald Frey later recalled, "It took something like five shots with the senior officers of the company to convince them to put money into the car." Although various designers, engineers, and executives did nurture the idea, without Iacocca's influence atop Dearborn's ivory tower, the Mustang would've never been born.

Iacocca's idea began taking shape not long after he became division general manager in November 1960. By the summer of 1961, Gene Bordinat's Advanced Styling Studio had already put a small, sporty model on paper. In May 1962, the Mustang I project commenced. A topless two-seater with a midships-mounted four-cylinder engine, the Mustang I was certainly intriguing, but it didn't mesh with Iacocca's plans for low-priced, wide-appeal, exciting-yet-practical transportation. "Up until that point," remembered Frey, "we had been thinking two-seaters. But [Iacocca] was right; there was a much bigger market for a four-seater."

Iacocca's challenge to his styling staff that summer to create a youthful four-seater produced rapid results. Although studio head Joe Oros is commonly credited with the shape, it was his assistant, Dave Ash, who designed the so-called "Cougar," a long-hood/short-deck styling proposition that went from clay to regular production in short order, with relatively few modifications. Familiar mockups were appearing by August 1962, followed in October 1963 by the prophetic Mustang II, a four-place showcar that demonstrated in no uncertain

If curbside critics thought the 1967 ponycar redesign was big news they had another thing coming in 1971 when the Mustang grew, somewhat alarmingly, on all fronts.

Compare this Grabber Yellow '71 Cobra Jet Mach 1 to its Signalflare Red '66 GT forerunner.

Long disappointed with the Mustang's direction after 1966, Lee Iacocca attempted to turn things around in 1974 by rolling out the little Mustang II. But while initial responses bordered on ecstatic, the idea quickly soured. And by 1978 the second-generation ponycar was history. Most prominent of this short-lived bloodline was the spoilered and striped '78 King Cobra.

terms that Ford had given up on the two-place ideal originally demonstrated by the Mustang I. Many among the sporting public were not pleased, however, especially those at *Motor Trend* who felt it was "a shame the Mustang name had to be diluted this way."

Such thoughts were quickly swept away by the flood of positive responses to Ford's all-new Mustang, introduced at the New York World's Fair as a midyear model, later to become known as a "1964-1/2" offering. *Car and Driver* called it "the best thing to come out of Dearborn since

Mustang performance really took off in the mid-'80s after more than a dozen years of Camaro dominance on Mainstreet U.S.A. A minor GT restyle in 1987 supplied the "aero" look while 225 horses worth of 5.0L V8 backed up that look with some serious muscle. This red GT convertible is a 1988 model. Other than a few minor changes—primarily wheels and tires—the Mustang exterior remained essentially unchanged up through 1993.

After rolling on the same "Fox chassis" platform for 14 years, Ford redesigned and totally restyled the Mustang for 1994. Underneath that attractive, modernized shell is, among other things, an exceptionally rigid chassis and standard four-wheel disc brakes. GT power still comes from the ever-present 5.0L small-block V8, now rated at 215 horses.

"The best thing to come out of Dearborn since the 1932 V-8 Model B roadster."

-Car and Driver

the 1932 V-8 Model B roadster." In the words of *Road & Track's* Gene Booth, the Mustang was "a car for the enthusiast who may be a family man, but likes his transportation to be more sporting."

Imagine that, a youthful, sporty flair in a practical, easy-to-handle package, all for around $2400. Bucket seats and floor shifter standard. Crisp, fresh styling that belied the cost-saving Falcon-based platform beneath the skin. Loads of options. Even more performance potential. Any way you looked at it, the new Mustang was many things to many people, some 417,000 people to be semi-exact. In base form with its economical six-cylinder engine, it was a practical, budget-minded grocery-getter that brought home the bacon in style. Go-getter was a better term for a Mustang armed with one of the hot optional V8s, which would only get hotter each year.

While power sources grew stronger, the Mustang grew as well, basically to make more room for more engine. A restyle for 1967 produced a wider, rounded body, but that was nothing compared to the longer, heavier, palatial pony intro-

duced for 1971. A large look that carried over into 1973 as sagging sales signalled the end for the first-generation Mustang. What followed was Iacocca's attempt to restore his original ideal, and the downsized Mustang II initially sold exceptionally well, then it too faded, lasting just five years through 1978. A totally redesigned "Fox-chassis" Mustang appeared the following year, kicking off the third generation, which managed to stay on the scene until 1993. And now we have yet another generation of Mustang, the totally redesigned SN-95 platform. What it was, it is, you can bet your spurs.

Thirty years and still running, how much longer is anyone's guess. One thing's for certain, though. Rivals and imposters may come and go, but there will always be only one Mustang, the progenitor of the long-hood/short-deck breed. Camaro, Firebird, you name it; regardless of the marque, there still all known as "ponycars."

As it did in 1964 and 1979, the latest, greatest all-new Mustang was chosen as the official pace car for the Indianapolis 500. Performing that duty at The Brickyard in May 1994 was a Special Vehicle Team Cobra, a car powered by a modified 240hp version of the 5.0L V8. This '94 SVT Cobra droptop was one of 1000 Indy Pace Car replicas built to mark the occasion. Adding the typical official decal to the door was up to the owner.

2 1964-1966

Off And Running On The Inside Track

While Ford's Mustang is credited with kicking off the ponycar breed, it wasn't exactly the first entrant in Detroit's long-hood/short-deck derby. That honor actually belongs to Plymouth's Barracuda, an equally small, sporty machine that beat the Mustang out of the gates by a couple weeks in April 1964. Basically a Valiant with a large, sloping rear window grafted on; the hastily created Barracuda didn't quite turn heads the way the Mustang did with its totally fresh image, a fact quickly demonstrated by the runaway lead Ford

Topless travel has always represented the only way to fly for the sporty set, and Ford Mustang buyers were no exception in 1966. Throw in a set of optional styled-steel wheels and the hot 271hp "Hi-Po" 289 V8 and the deal was irresistible. Notice this rare Hi-Po convertible is not a GT.

took in the early ponycar sales race. As total Mustang production was zooming past 500,000 into the car's second year, Plymouth was moving 23,443 '64 Barracudas, followed by another 64,596 in 1965.

Of course more competition would come soon enough. By late 1966, General Motors was rolling out its own ponycars, Chevrolet's Camaro and Pontiac's Firebird, while Mercury was letting its luxurious Cougar run free in the Ford Motor Company corral. A year later, even American Motors was entering the race, introducing its Javelin and two-seat AMX as 1968 models. But for nearly the first two and a half years of its life, Ford's wildly popular Mustang basically ran unopposed, a situation Iacocca had planned all along.

Ford's all-new breed debuted on April 17, 1964, as a "notchback" coupe and a sexy

Ford's Mustang was by no means the first to demonstrate the long-hood/short-deck theme—consider Chevrolet's Corvette, Studebaker's Avanti and Ford's own two-seat Thunderbirds of 1955-57—but may well stand today as the car best recognized for fitting the profile to a T. While all first-year Mustangs sold between April 1964 and August 1965 were originally referred to as 1965 models, the early run ending in August 1964 was soon labeled "'64-1/2." This '64-1/2 coupe features Pagoda Green paint, one of five shades only offered on those early Mustangs. Also notice the "260" fender badge. The optional 164hp 260cid 2V (two-barrel carburetor) V8 was traded for a 200hp 289cid 2V Windsor small-block after the so-called '64-1/2 production ended.

convertible. An idea basically "borrowed" from Chevrolet's Corvair Monza, the standard combination of bucket seats and a floor shifter established the Mustang's sporty feel, regardless of which engine was beneath that long hood. And although a Falcon-style instrument panel served as a reminder that much of the structure beneath the Mustang's skin was passed up from Ford's little econo-buggy, most who took a seat behind that racy three-spoke steering wheel couldn't have cared less.

Desirable options, both factory-supplied or dealer installed, were plentiful,

Helping enhance the Mustang's sporty image were standard bucket seats and a floor shifter. A console was optional, as was underdash air conditioning. Integral in-dash air conditioning wouldn't be incorporated into the design until 1967. Base Mustangs (non-GTs and those without the optional deluxe Interior Decor group) built prior to 1966 can also be identified by their simple Falcon-based instrument panel.

including typical amenities like power steering and brakes, underdash air conditioning, a power top for convertibles, and Ford's three-speed Cruise-O-Matic automatic transmission. Sport-minded buyers could've also added a four-speed stick, an interior console, the popular "Rally Pac" (a column-mounted tachometer/clock combo), a special handling package (heavy-duty suspension), and the attrac-

tive styled-steel 14-inch five-spoke wheels. Also helping dress things up outside was a vinyl roof and various simulated wire wheelcovers.

Base power came from a 101hp 170cid six-cylinder powerplant, replaced that fall by a stronger, more durable 200cid six, rated at 120 horses. Optional V8s included the Falcon's 164hp 260 with a two-barrel carburetor and its slightly larger Windsor small-block brother, the 210-horse 289, fed by a four-barrel. The 260 V8 was soon dropped, replaced by a 200hp 289 two-barrel once the so-called '64-1/2 Mustang gave way to "true" 1965 production in August 1964. A higher-compression 225hp 289 four-barrel V8 was also added, superseding the original 210hp 289.

Listed in April 1964 but not available until June 1, the truly hot High Performance 289 joined the Mustang lineup late, then instantly hit the ground running. Special heads, a potent solid-lifter cam, a 600-cfm Autolite four-barrel breathing through a chrome open-element air cleaner, beefed main bearing caps on the block's lower end, a mechanical-advance distributor, and free-breathing exhaust manifolds helped set the "Hi-Po" 289 apart from the herd. Compression was 10.5:1 while the all-important output figure was advertised at 271 horsepower.

The Hi-Po 289 was just the kick the new ponycar needed. *Road & Track*'s crit-

ics called the 271hp Mustang a "four-passenger Cobra." Equally impressed were *Car Life's* testers, who lauded the Hi-Po for its "obvious superiority to the more mundane everyday Mustang." Continued *Car Life's* September 1964 report, "where the latter has a style and a flair of design that promises a road-hugging sort

When introduced in April 1964, the Mustang offered three power choices: the standard 101hp 170cid six-cylinder and two Windsor small-block V8s, the 164hp 260 2V and this 289 4V, rated at 210 horsepower. The optional 271hp "Hi-Po" 289 appeared in June, while the three original engines were replaced later that fall; the 170 six by a 200cid version, the 260 V8 by a 200hp 289 2V, and the 210hp 289 by the 225hp 289 4V. Notice the generator (just above the battery) on this 210hp 289; it represents one of the easiest ways to identify a '64-1/2 Mustang. Later models used alternators.

Pedal Cars

Feet Don't Fail Me Now

Frenzied car buyers weren't the only ones to notice Dearborn's enormously popular Mustang in the spring of 1964. About the time Iacocca and crew were rushing their ponycar project to market, toymakers at the American Machine and Foundry Company (AMF), in Olney, Illinois, were putting together their own plan to jump on the Mustang bandwagon—with both feet. Presented to Iacocca by AMF's Patrick Wilkins were three prototype vehicles, truly small cars intended for truly youthful drivers. Ford's vice president liked the idea, and thus the Mustang pedal car was born.

Sold through Ford dealers, AMF's "Midget Mustang" pedal car appeared just in time for Christmas 1964. Full-page ads in at least a half dozen major magazines announced the Midget Mustang's debut to the kids while also enticing mom and dad to put themselves behind the wheel of a somewhat larger, fossile-fuel-fired ponycar convertible. Price for the pedal-driven variety was $12.95.

Mustang pedal cars stood only 14 inches tall, rolled on a 23-inch wheelbase, and measured 39 inches front to rear. Whitewall rubber tires were standard, as were deluxe wheelcovers and a steel three-spoke steering wheel, items all modelled after the real things. Additional sporty features included a Rally-Pac instrument cluster decal and a workable three-speed stick mounted atop the righthand door. Although rumors claim a few Midget Mustangs may have been painted light blue/grey, all Ford-marketed pedal cars were red, at least originally. Many were soon repainted to match dad's full-sized Mustang.

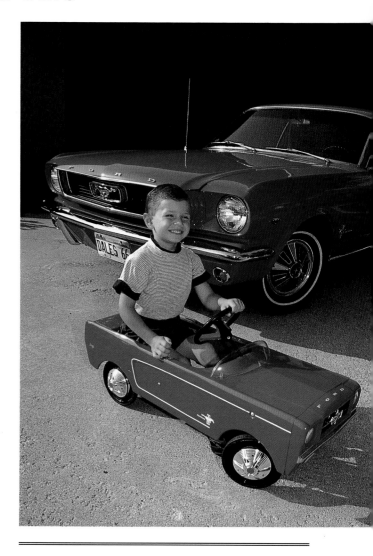

Introduced just in time for Christmas 1964, AMF's Midget Mustang pedal cars were sold through Ford dealers up through 1965. Although rumors of light blue examples exist, all were apparently red with rubber tires and a stickshift on the passenger door. Many were later repainted to match dad and mom's full-sized ponycar.

Another variation involved the limited-edition Indianapolis 500 Pace Car pedal cars distributed earlier to the Indy 500 Festival Committee. Appropriately painted white with a blue stripe down the hood and decklid and wearing bodyside decals, these pedal-powered pacers featured a hand-lettered serial number tag beneath the skin. Reportedly, only 100 were produced, with maybe four still known today, one bringing a then-record $1,700 at a recent collector auction.

Ford dealers continued selling the Midget Mustangs through the 1965 Christmas season, then Dearborn decided to drop the promotion in 1966. AMF wasn't deterred, however, and continued marketing the Mustang pedal car—sans official Ford Motor Company logos—on its own before ending production in 1972. Various minor changes were made during that span, the most notable being a switch from red paint to yellow in 1971.

According to toy expert Ken Schmidt, owner of Indianapolis' Blue Diamond Classics, a leading parts source and restorer of Mustang pedal cars, AMF built 110,812

That $12.95 asking price wasn't exactly cheap for a toy in 1964, but it pales in comparison to the amounts paid by collectors today, totals sometimes surpassing $1000. AMF continued manufacturing its Mustang pedal cars even after Ford dropped support after 1965. Later models were devoid of official Ford identification and were painted yellow beginning in 1971. Production ended the following year.

kid-powered ponycar convertibles, all using the same stamped steel body modeled after the original Mustang. After ceasing production in 1972, AMF sold its tooling to the CIA Corporation in Mexico City, Mexico, where Mustang pedal cars production resumed, this time in various colors. Another attempt to revive the breed came in 1984 when The Little Car Company of San Diego attempted to import 1000 pedal cars from the Mexican firm to help commemorate the Mustang's 25th anniversary. Poor quality, however, hindered the effort and only 200 were actually distributed among U.S. dealers.

Whether built in Mexico or Illinois, all Mustang pedal cars are valued collectibles today. Schmidt claims a CIA-marketed car, new in its box, is worth about $650, while pristine AMF-produced examples have sold for twice that price. Blue Diamond Classics asks as much as $1000 to restore well-used Midget Mustangs. Clearly, playing with Mustang pedal cars can no longer be considered a kid's game.

Easily the most valuable of the Mustang pedal car herd is this Indy Pace Car replica, one of maybe 100 specially serial-numbered toys distributed among the Indianapolis 500 Festival Committee in May 1964. Only about four of these are known today, according to Blue Diamond Classics' Ken Schmidt of Indianapolis, perhaps this country's leading Mustang pedal car restoration expert.

of performance and then falls slightly short of this self-established goal, the HP Mustang backs up its looks in spades." Quoted quarter-mile time for a Hi-Po Mustang with a 3.89:1 differential was 15.9 seconds at 85 mph. *Car and Driver's*

hotfoots pushed the envelope even further with a 271hp Mustang motivated by 4.11:1 rear gears, managing a sizzling 14-second quarter-mile pass at 100 mph.

Three months after the impressive Hi-Po 289 appeared, Ford enhanced the

Also introduced in the fall of 1964 was a third Mustang bodystyle, the sexy 2+2 fastback. This '65 2+2 features upscale optional wire wheelcovers. But since its fenders wear no badges, underhood power comes from a budget-minded base six-cylinder.

Mustang's sporty image another notch with a third bodystyle, the "2+2" fastback, officially introduced September 9, 1964. With its seductive, sweeping roofline and similarly effective fold-down rear seat, the Mustang 2+2 was an instant crowd favorite, drawing more than 77,000 buyers in 1965.

Ponycar customers who wanted even more pizzazz, performance, and prestige were surely pleased with two more optional packages introduced in April 1965 to mark the Mustang's one-year anniversary. The interior decor group, more affectionately now known as the "pony interior" for the running horses embossed into the seat inserts, spruced up things inside considerably. Along with those intriguing seat inserts—used both front and rear—the pony interior also included luxury door panels, a simulated walnut rim for the steering wheel, pistol-grip door handles, a five-dial instrument panel, various bright mouldings, more simulated walnut here and there, and door-mounted red-and-white courtesy lights. Although the interior decor option was available for all three bodystyles, a fastback received a slightly different version as the fold-down rear seat did not have the pony inserts.

While the pony interior wowed 'em inside, the other April 1965 addition to the Mustang options list turned heads in more ways than one. Featuring both a hefty dose of eye-catching exterior ima-

This larger, beefier 120hp 200cid six-cylinder replaced the original 101hp 170 six in the fall of 1964. Revised features included seven main bearings, a new cam, bigger valves, and higher compression, 9.2:1 compared to 8.7:1. Base six-cylinder sales made up 35.6 percent of 1965 Mustang production.

gery and a heaping helping of heavy-duty hardware, the GT equipment group was just the ticket for those among the ponycar faithful who wanted it all— sporty looks and gutsy performance. Available with the 225- and 271-horse 289 V8s only, the GT group included power front disc brakes and the special handling package, which added stiffer springs, bigger shocks, quicker 22:1 steering (standard steering was 27:1), and a thicker front stabilizer bar. GT Mustangs were

Previous page: Along with special "2+2" fender emblems, '65 Mustang fastbacks also received chrome rocker mouldings as standard equipment—they were optional for coupes and convertibles. Also notice the lack of trim within the simulated rear-quarter vent. Fastback and GTs in 1965 and '66 didn't have this trim, while coupes and convertibles did. Optional styled-steel wheels for 1965 were fully chromed while the same type sport wheel in 1966 featured only a bright center section with a chromed trim ring covering the unplated rim.

also adorned with appropriate fender badges, lower bodyside stripes, grille-mounted fog lamps, and twin exhaust trumpets exiting through the rear valance. The optional four-speed, limited-slip differential, and styled-steel wheels would've been icing on the cake as far as supreme GT performance was concerned in 1965 and '66. Was there a better way to fly?

Perhaps not. Then again, not all Mustangers looked to the sky. Budget-conscious, economical ponycars were far more plentiful than their high-flying, high-profile GT cousins, and this plain truth wasn't overlooked by Dearborn's gay marketeers.

As part of an early 1966 sales push centered around the upcoming produc-tion of the millionth Mustang, Ford put together yet another special ponycar, this one geared towards promoting the yeo-man six-cylinder models. Offered as a hardtop convertible and rarely seen fast-back, the Sprint 200 Mustang featured bodyside accent pinstripes, wire wheel-covers, an interior console, and a chrome air cleaner with an appropriate decal atop the 200cid six beneath the hood. Sure, it wasn't all that awe-inspiring, but the Sprint 200 did demonstrate that practical-ity didn't necessarily have to be dull, something Mustang dealers already knew.

After rolling out nearly 700,000 Mus-tangs during the extended 1965 model run beginning in April 1964, Ford fol-lowed up with some 607,000 more in 1966. Not wanting to break something that didn't need fixing, Dearborn design-ers barely touched their second-edition ponycar, letting the same shell return in 1966, showing only minor trim changes here and there. With demand being so great, who cared?

Optional equipment on this '66 coupe includes the black vinyl top, styled-steel wheels, GT equipment group and High-Performance 289 V8. Introduced in April 1965 to help mark the Mustang's first anniversary, the GT package included a nice array of image and performance pieces, including twin foglamps in a blacked-out grille, "GT" fender emblems, lower bodyside stripes, front discs, heavy-duty suspension and dual exhausts exiting through cutouts in the rear valance. Adding the optional K-code "Hi-Po" 289 only helped sweeten the GT pot even further. Hi-Po Mustangs received standard redline tires unless superseded by optional whitewalls, as is the case with the red 271hp convertible shown in this chapter.

Right: Rated at 271 horsepower, the Hi-Po 289 was the hottest Mustang powerplant available from its debut in June 1964 up until the 390cid big-block V8 appeared as a Mustang option in 1967. Although still offered that year, few 271hp 289s found their way beneath '67 Mustang hoods. As in 1965, the '66 Hi-Po shown here features chrome dress-up and an open-element air cleaner. Special valvetrain gear and beefier connecting rods and main bearing caps made the Hi-Po 289 a high-winding demon. Maximum power came on at 6000 rpm and 7000 revs were no problem.

Introduced along with the GT equipment group in April 1965, the Interior Decor package added deluxe appointments inside, including these attractive "running horse" seat inserts. Called the "pony interior," *this option carried over almost unchanged into 1966, with the main difference being the five-dial instrument panel included as part of the deal in 1965. It was already standard on all models the following year.*

3 1967-1970

From Polite Pony to Bucking Bronco

Perhaps the best combination of ponycar car pizzazz and performance, the Mach 1 Mustang debuted to rave reviews in 1969. "Are you ready for the first great Mustang?" asked a Car Life report. "One with performance to match its looks, handling to send imported-car fans home mumbling to themselves, and an interior as elegant and livable as a gentleman's club?" Inside the Mach 1 "SportsRoof" were high-back buckets, a sport steering wheel, a console, and lots of simulated woodgrain. Outside were various dress-up features, like a blacked-out hood, non-functional scoop, racing-type hood pins, color-keyed racing mirrors, a pop-open gas cap, and chromed styled-steel wheels. Engine choice varied; this '69 Mach 1 is powered by the top-dog 335hp 428 Cobra Jet with functional ram-air, a powerful package representing suitable symmetry for the equally intimidating North-American P-51 fighter plane in the background.

Like many ponycar purists then and now, Lee Iacocca never did approve of the new direction taken by his pet project in 1967. "Within a few years after its introduction," he later wrote in his autobiography, "the Mustang was no longer a sleek horse, it was more like a fat pig."

Indeed, Iacocca's once-petite baby did grow some in time for the 1967 model year. Length stretched 2in, width increased by more than 2.5 inches, and height went up a 0.5in. While the new model's wheelbase remained at 108 inches, both front and rear tracks were widened to 58 inches, from 55.4 and 56, respectively. And of course all this up-sizing meant more weight too, about 130 lbs worth. Exterior styling swelled as well; in place of the earlier crisp, light lines was a bulging, rounded facade.

Lee Iacocca, the so-called father of the Mustang, didn't like the 1967 restyle at all, nor did he approve of the prime motivation behind rounding and widening the ponycar's flanks—to make room for the big-block 390 GT V8. Nonetheless, the restyled look was certainly not lacking in attractiveness. Even with the new concave taillight cove, twin-vented hood and revised measurements, much of the original Mustang image carried over. And again, GT models represented the top of the ponycar heap.

Obesity, however, is in the eye of the beholder. Not everyone agreed with Iacocca, and no one in 1967 was by any means ready to write the Mustang off as a great idea gone bad. Detractors, in fact, were in the minority as buyers continued flocking to Ford dealers in droves, inspired in part by the soothing words of *Hot Rod's* Eric Dahlquist. "Detroit has cobbled up so many fine designs in the last 20 years that when Ford decided to change the Mustang, everybody held their breath," wrote Dahlquist in *HRM's* March 1967 issue. "But it's okay, people, everythin's gonna' be all right."

As for why Ford had decided to change the Mustang, to fix something that on the surface didn't appear to need fixing, the answer involved rolling stones. Among others, Hal Sperlich, Donald Frey's special projects assistant, didn't want to see Ford's all-new ponycar gather moss. Even as the first Mustangs were being bought at a record pace in 1964, Sperlich was looking ahead to what everyone hoped would be a bigger, better model.

As chief Mustang product planner Ross Humphries later told author Gary Witzenburg in 1978, "Hal's feeling was that in the past when we had brought out a new car that was a winner, we had rested on our laurels and didn't do enough to upgrade the car to keep the momentum going. And soon our friends across town would come back and do us one better.

In order to fit the big 390cid FE-series big-block V8 beneath a '67 Mustang's long hood, designers had to rearrange the shock towers to supply enough side-to-side clearance. Fed by a four-barrel carburetor, the 390 GT V8 was rated at 320 horsepower. GT Mustangs in 1967 could've been equipped with the 390 big-block or 289 small-block.

Hal's philosophy on the '67 Mustang was to one-up the original in every respect without making a major change."

Engineering changes beneath the skin involved improving ride and handling by revamping the basic platform and front suspension, which was also widened to make room for more engine beneath the hood. Basically, it was the "more engine" that made for more Mustang in 1967.

A new option for 1967 was this tilt steering wheel that, along with adjusting to nine different driving positions, would automatically swing up and away towards the center of the interior once the driver's door was opened. Also notice the optional in-dash air conditioning (vents above the radio) and stylish full console with storage compartment, both new for 1967. Optional speed control was introduced that year as well.

Mechanical parameters and sheetmetal simply had to expand to allow engineers to drop Ford's FE-series big-block V8 into the Mustang, a move that more or less had to happen if Dearborn wanted to stay at the head of the ponycar pack.

Although somewhat slow in coming, General Motors' ponycar spin-offs finally appeared in late 1966, and both Chevrolet's '67 Camaro and Pontiac's '67 Firebird hit the ground running hard, each with an optional high-powered big-block V8, Chevy's 396 and PMD's 400. To keep up, Ford let loose its first big-block Mustang, powered by the 320-horse 390 FE V8, offered with or without the GT equipment group. Also listed for '67 Mustang GTs only was Ford's former top-dog ponycar powerplant, the 271hp Hi-Po 289 small-block, making its final appearance.

A new twist for 1967 involved Mustang GT transmission choices. Choosing the optional Select-Shift Cruise-O-Matic automatic transmission added a red-accented "A" to the GT emblem. All "GT" models were equipped with manual transmissions, while all "GTA" Mustangs had automatics. Although a neat little identification trick, the GTA did not carry over into 1968.

In base form, the new-look '67 Mustang remained a budget-conscious sportabout with six-cylinder power. But Ford promotional men were more than proud of their equally new power lineup, now made up of 13 different engine/transmission combi-

An identification trick used only in 1967 involved the GT Mustang's transmission. While a manual-trans '67 GT was simply a GT, those equipped with the Select-Shift Cruise-O-Matic automatic received a red "A" on their fenders. All GTs in 1967 had sticks, all automatic cars were "GTA" models. This GTA convertible is powered by a 225hp 289 4V V8.

nations. Six-cylinder, small-block or big-block, three-speed, four-speed or automatic; it was in there. So were various structural enhancements and new options like a tilt-away steering wheel, cruise control, a folding glass convertible top window, and fully integrated in-dash air conditioning. A one-up on the original? *Motor Trend's* John Ethridge thought so, claiming "just about every Mustang change for '67 seems to bring the car closer to our notion of a true Grand Touring machine."

From a top performance perspective, however, not all was well in 1967. Even with the 390 big-block, a '67 Mustang GT was still no match for a 396 Camaro SS or Firebird 400. Using a fast-food analogy in reference to the 390 GT, *Car Life's* curbside critics suggested that "perhaps this super-burger, if it is to be a superburger, needs a little more mustard."

Ready with a jar of French's was renowned East Coast Ford dealer Robert F. Tasca of East Providence, Rhode Island.

Among noticeable exterior revisions for 1968 was different grille trim, "Mustang" fender script instead of block fenders, revised trim again for those fake rear-quarter vents, and totally redesigned optional styled steel wheels. When included along with the GT equipment, those chromed wheels wore center caps with large "GT" identification.

One of the country's most prominent promoters of Blue Oval performance, Bob Tasca was certainly no stranger to making Fords go fast, both at the dragstrip and on the street. But while Ford's so-called "Total Performance" campaign, originally initiated in 1963, had produced a worldwide race-winning reputation for Dearborn, regular-production performance available to Tasca and other dealers quickly fell well behind the competition. Tasca began noticing the shortfall in 1966.

"We did well from '63 to '65, when the car-buying market was a young one," Bob Tasca told *Super Stock* in 1968. Then "the younger people [became] disenchanted with Ford's performance on the street, and stopped buying." Reportedly, Detroit sold 634,434 high-performance cars (those with more than 300 horsepower) in 1966. Ford's

Ford put the Mustang on the musclecar map in April 1968, introducing the fabled 428 Cobra Jet variety. With 335 CJ horses between its flanks and the complete array of GT equipment throughout, the '68-1/2 Cobra Jet Mustang was a winner on the street, while on the run or standing still. This CJ Mustang was originally sold at Tasca Ford in East Providence, Rhode Island, the "birthplace" of the 428 Cobra Jet. It was Bob Tasca's men who in 1967 first began experimenting with mixing and matching Ford FE-series big-block parts to make the Mustang more competitive on the street performance scene.

piece of that performance pie? A mere 7.5 percent. "Shameful for a 'Total Performance' company," said Tasca.

Ford's first big-block Mustang did little to ease that shame. As Tasca Ford performance manager Dean Gregson told *Hot Rod's* Dahlquist in late 1967, "we sold a lot of 390 Mustangs last fall and into the winter, but by March they dropped off to practically nothing. That's when the snow melted off the asphalt." Continued Gregson, "we found the car so non-competitive we began to feel we were cheating the customer."

The 335hp Cobra Jet was based on a 428 passenger car block but included 427 low-riser heads, a cast-iron version of Ford's aluminum Police Interceptor (PI) intake mounting a big 735cfm Holley four-barrel, a 390 GT cam, PI rods, 10.6:1 pistons, low-restriction exhausts, and functional ram-air. Power front discs, braced shock towers, staggered rear shocks (on four-speed models), and a beefy 9-inch rearend were also included in the deal.

That summer, Tasca had taken it on himself to make the new big-block Mustang more competitive using parts right off the Ford shelf. Instead of the 390 FE, Tasca's men tried a 428 Police Interceptor V8 using big-valve heads and a 735-cfm Holley four-barrel. Presto, an instant 13.39-second quarter-mile sizzler. Soon after seeing Tasca's so-called "KR" Mustang—KR for King of the Road—Ford officials decided to build a regular-production counterpart, exchanged the KR designation for "Cobra Jet," and introduced the 428 CJ Mustang on April 1, 1968. Conservatively rated at 335 horsepower, the Tasca-inspired 428 Cobra Jet appeared just in time to save Ford's bacon on the street performance scene.

Looking much like one of Carroll Shelby's variants, the '68 California Special Mustang was a special promotional model put together by the Southern California Ford Dealers using many Shelby components. Offered only in GT coupe form with a six-cylinder as standard, the GT/CS featured a blacked-out grille with Lucas foglamps, twin hood locks, non-functional Shelby rear-quarter scoops, various striping, and "California Special" script in back. All engines were optional for the California Special.

Win On Sunday, Sell On Monday

Any Ford performance fan worth his salt knows the name Tasca. Tasca Ford, owned and operated by Robert F. Tasca Sr., was a mecca for East Coast Blue Oval horsepower hounds in the '60s. If it was hot and powered by Ford, you could've found it at 777 Taunton Avenue in East Providence, Rhode Island, from Cobras to Shelbys to 427 Galaxies to Mustang GTs. And parts, too. If it made Fords go fast, Bob Tasca—"the Bopper"—sold it.

Tasca Ford also raced it. The Bopper may not have been the first to recognize the relationship between sizzling victories at the track and hot sales on the street, but he was the man who coined the phrase, "win on Sunday, sell on Monday." Tasca Ford did both in spades, beginning in 1962 when the dealership's special competition department was formed, headed by Dean Gregson. Ace mechanics included John Healy and Ralph Poirier, who still works for The Bopper today.

Driver Bill Lawton joined the team soon afterward and drag racing victories quickly followed. Pilot-

Robert F. Tasca today at his home in Rhode Island with his 1930 Model A, a present from his three sons on his 65th birthday in October 1991. Once the "mascot" car at Georgia Tech, Tasca's Model A was restored at Ford's Atlanta plant.

The Tasca tradition continues—Bobby Tasca III stands proudly with his '92 Mustang, also a birthday present, in this case for the younger Tasca's 16th anniversary. Specially prepared both on the Ford line and at Jack Roush's shop, Tasca's GT is powered by a 400hp 340cid small-block put together at Tasca Lincoln-Mercury in Seekonk, Massachusetts. At the track, Bobby Tasca's Mustang will do 12.2 seconds in the quarter, topping out at 113mph.

ing Tasca Ford's '64 Thunderbolt, Lawton won top Super Stock honors at the National Hot Rod Association's 1964 Winternationals in Pomona, California. Lawton won again at the 1965 NHRA Winternationals, this time in Tasca's '65 A/FX Mustang. Between 1962 and '68, Bob Tasca spent nearly $300,000 racing, a wise investment considering the national exposure helped his dealership grow into this country's second leading Ford dealer.

Although a strong racing presence did greatly contribute to that rise, so too did Bob Tasca's mar-

keting expertise, his attention to details and his drive to be the best. A "grease monkey" at age 17, Tasca had first gone to work in May 1943 for Sandager Ford in Cranston, Rhode Island. By 1948, he had climbed the ladder to sales manager, then to general manager the following year. In November 1953, he opened his own dealership, making customer satisfaction his top priority, as it still is four decades later. As one Tasca employee put it, "Bob Tasca will do whatever it takes, whatever the cost to satisfy a customer—he will not quit until that guy leaves here happy."

Today, Bob Tasca's office is in Seekonk, Massachusetts, just a few blocks east of where the old Tasca Ford dealership used to be before it closed down in 1971. No, Tasca didn't go out of business, he just changed gears, trading Fords for Lincolns and Mercurys. And of course, not one Lincoln-Mercury dealer in the world does it better than Seekonk's Tasca Lincoln-Mercury, run by a second generation of Tascas, sons Robert Jr, Carl and David.

It's somewhat ironic. Robert F. Tasca Sr. first got his Rhode Island dealership rolling around 1960 by dressing up Fords with special custom luxury features. Once horsepower became the going thing, he began using that tool to promote high-powered sales, during which time he was directly responsible for Ford Motor Company's introduction of its street performance savior, the Cobra Jet Mustang, in April 1968. Once the musclecar era began to fade in 1971, Tasca left his hot rod days behind, with no regrets, and returned to the world of luxury cars. He has alway been one to look ahead, not behind. Win on Sunday? Robert F. Tasca wins every day.

According to Tasca, "the Cobra Jet began the era of Ford's performance supremacy. In my opinion, it was the fastest production car in the world at that point. And I'm not talking top speed, I'm talking fun fast, get up and go." After witnessing a pre-production Cobra Jet run the quarter-mile in a sensational 13.56 seconds, *Hot Rod's* ever-present Dahlquist couldn't have agreed more, claiming "the CJ will be the utter delight of every Ford lover and the bane of all the rest because, quite frankly, it is probably the fastest regular production sedan ever built."

Mustang performance heated up even more in 1969, the year for yet another restyled ponycar body. That new look was certainly hot, as were a handful of new models, muscular Mustangs that appeared thanks mostly to the earlier arrival of Semon E. "Bunkie" Knudsen. On February 6, 1968, Henry Ford II had shocked Detroit—and Lee Iacocca—by hiring Knudsen, GM's former executive vice president, as Ford's president. Knudsen loved performance, and under his direction Mustang performance flourished.

Bunkie's logic was simple. In his opinion, the Mustang was "a good-looking automobile, but there are a tremendous number of people out there who want good-looking automobiles with performance. If a car looks like it's going fast and doesn't go fast, people get turned off. You should give the sports-minded fellow the opportunity to buy a high-performance automobile." That he did. Three new high-performance Mustangs debuted during Knudsen's brief 18-month stay atop Ford, the Mach 1, Boss 302 and Boss 429.

At the tail, the California Special was adorned with the Shelby's fiberglass ducktail decklid and sequential turn-signal Thunderbird taillights. Although the letters "GT" were used as part of the California Special's name, the cars weren't GTs unless equipped with that options package, which of course added, among other things, quad exhaust tips and a set of 14x6 styled-steel wheels. Total California Special production, including the 300 similar "High Country Specials" sold out of Denver, was 4,325 cars.

It's called a "Shaker," and for good reason. The optional ram-air equipment introduced for the Mustang in 1969 protruded right through the hood, vibrating for all to see whenever a 428 Cobra Jet's pedal went to the metal. A '69 CJ Mach 1 became the "quickest four-place production car" ever tested by Car Life, running the quarter-mile in 13.9 seconds.

The most civilized of the three, at least in standard form, the '69 Mach 1 "SportsRoof" (Ford's new name for its fastbacks) was many cars to many drivers, depending on the chosen underhood power source. A 351cid two-barrel Windsor small-block was standard, with optional engines including a four-barrel 351, the 320hp 390 GT big-block, and proven 335hp 428 Cobra Jet, with or without that distinctive ram-air "Shaker" hood scoop.

Whatever the engine, a Mach 1 made its presence known thanks to a whole host of standard sporty features. Blacked-out hood with non-functional scoop (unless ram-air was specified). Racing-type hood pins and dual color-keyed rac-

Reportedly, Ford only built 13 428 CJ convertibles for 1969, and this is the only known example with a ram-air Cobra Jet backed by a four-speed, the latter included as part of the Drag Pack option.

Transforming a Cobra Jet into a Super Cobra Jet, the Drag Pack added an oil cooler, a Top-Loader four-speed and a 4.30:1 Traction-Lok 9-inch rearend.

ing mirrors. "Mach 1" bodyside stripes. Pop-open gas cap. Chrome styled steel wheels. "Special Handling" suspension with E70 rubber. And that wasn't all. Inside, high-back buckets, a sport steering wheel, console, and simulated woodgrain appointments were also made part of the deal; a package that so impressed *Car Life's* editors, they named the new Mach 1 their "Best Ponycar" for 1969.

Mustang buyers were also impressed, or at least the 72,458 who chose '69 Mach 1s were. Another 40,970 customers bought Mach 1s the following year, when the equally impressive 351 Cleveland small-block joined the Mustang options list.

More purposeful and less likely to appeal to the average ponycar buyer, Bunkie's two Boss Mustangs stood at opposite ends of the performance spectrum. One was a high-winding small-block screamer, slung low to handle like nobody's business. The other was a nose-heavy, cantankerous big-block beast, built to run in a straight line, preferably a line measuring exactly one quarter mile.

Ford's Boss 302 was created in response to Knudsen's demand for "absolutely the best-handling street car available on the American market," an appropriate goal considering the plan was to take the car racing on the Sports Car Club of America's Trans Am circuit. Chassis engineer Matt Donner responded with a lowered, heavy-duty suspension and fat F60 tires on seven-inch-wide wheels. Designer Larry Shinoda, another GM refugee who followed Knudsen to Ford, supplied the spoilers, slats, and splashy graphics. And power came from an exclusive 290hp 302cid small-block topped by Ford's excellent canted-valve Cleveland heads. Brute force, however, wasn't the idea here. Wouldn't you know it, according to *Car and Driver* the Boss 302 Mustang was "the best handling Ford ever to come out of Dearborn and may just be the new standard by which everything from Detroit must be judged." Boss 302 production was 1,934 for 1969, another 6,318 for 1970.

Brute force, on the other hand, *was* the Boss 429's forte. Also unique to its application, the 375hp "semi-hemi" Boss 429 big-block was actually created to make the

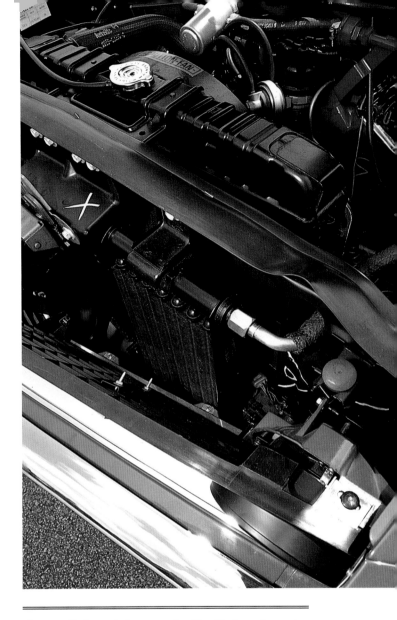

Super Cobra Jets were built with hard use in mind, and were thus beefed on the bottom end to keep the crank and rods where they belonged. Also assisting in holding this hell-raiser together was this external oil cooler, mounted just ahead of the radiator on the driver's side.

Boss 302 Mustangs, built in both 1969 and '70, simply can't be missed on the street, thanks in part to their low-slung stance, those various radiant paint schemes, and that reflective bodyside stripe. This Grabber Blue '70 Boss 302 was one of 6,318 built. The Magnum 500 wheels, rear spoiler, and window slats were optional equipment.

Right: Although road handling was the Boss 302's forte, it was also no slouch under the hood, where 290 horses supplied by a canted-valve, Cleveland-head 302 small-block were ready, willing, and able to wind out all day long. But just in case a driver did a little too much winding, a 6150-rpm rev limiter (barely visible in silver just to the right and below the power steering pump's dipstick) was included as part of the package. The ram-air Shaker scoop was a Boss 302 option in 1970.

rounds on NASCAR's stock car racing circuit behind the extended snout of Ford's '69 Talladega but had to be homologated in a regular-production model before it could legally compete. NASCAR rules only asked that 500 street-worthy examples of an eligible racing engine be built; they didn't specify the particular model those engines had to go into. So the Boss 429 V8 was homologated for the NASCAR-spec Talladegas by being offered as an option for '69 Mustangs.

Clearly a race engine not intended for the street, the big, brawny Boss 429 with its huge ports wasn't exactly suited for everyday operation. Even though it could propel a Mustang to mid-13-second bursts through the quarter-mile, that performance was still below potential. In Shinoda's words, the semi-hemi 429 "was kind of a slug in the Mustang." Slug or not, Boss 429s attracted 859 buyers in 1969, followed by 499 more before production ceased in January 1970.

Almost lost in the two Boss Mustangs' shadows, the once-prominent GT made its final appearance in 1969. Production was only 5,396, the lowest total during

Hands down, the most beastly Mustang ever was the Boss 429, a hunkered-down, hairy animal with a heavy-duty lowered suspension, big 15-inch Magnum 500 wheels and 375 horses worth of "semi-hemi" V8 beneath a huge hood scoop. Scoops on '69 Boss 429s were painted to match the body, while '70 scoops were black. This Grabber Blue '70 Boss 429 was among 499 built. Another 859 had rolled down the Kar Kraft production line in Brighton, Michigan, the year before.

the five-year run. And while the GT was on its way out in 1969, the upscale Grande was making its first appearance. Offered in hardtop form only, the Mustang Grande featured wire wheelcovers, a deluxe interior, and various insulation and suspension upgrades to guarantee a quieter ride. A standard vinyl landau roof and houndstooth cloth seats were added to the package for 1970. Grande hardtop sales hit 22,182 in 1969, 13,581 the following year.

A luxury ponycar? Perhaps the times they were a-changin'. Again.

"The Boss 429 started out as a NASCAR engine. We were going to build enough to make it legal for NASCAR. In order to make it racing legal, we had to sell them. The bottom end was similar to the Super Cobra jet 429. The Boss 429 Hemi-head was really patterned after the Chrysler Hemi, to tell you the truth. The hemispherical combustion chamber still is the best from a power standpoint and surface-to-volume ratio."
—Hank Lennox, Ford Engineer

Interestingly, the Boss 429 V8 was made a Mustang option only to homologate the engine as a NASCAR-legal racing powerplant for Ford's aerodynamic long-nose Talladega. NASCAR Talladegas had Boss 429s behind their odd-looking snouts; street Talladegas used 428 Cobra Jets. Fitting the big 375hp semi-hemi V8 into a Mustang engine bay required moving the shock towers one inch farther apart. Ram-air equipment and a 735cfm Holley four-barrel were standard.

What's In A Name?

As Ford's famous galloping logo implies, a Mustang is a horse, a "wild horse of the North American plains" to be exact per most dictionaries. But while making the obvious connection between pony and car is simple enough, that's not exactly how Iacocca's baby was originally christened, at least not according to executive stylist John Najjar. Although the name did indeed initially come right off a North American plane, that was plane as in airplane. And North American as in North American Aviation, Inc., builders of the legendary P-51 Mustang fighter of World War II.

It seems Najjar had a thing for the awesome P-51, among the world's best performing fighter aircraft before the arrival of jet technology made prop power obsolete immediately following the war's end in 1945. Even then, Mustangs were ready, willing and able to take to the air in anger again five years later when hostilities broke out in Korea, then continued flying for various foreign air forces, seeing additional action as late as 1956 for Israel against Egypt. Over the years since, Mustangs have remained "in action" as airshow stars and dominating air-racers.

In all, some 15,300 P-51s were built beginning in 1941 at North American's plants in Inglewood, California, and Dallas, Texas. Initially underpowered and ceiling restricted with an unsupercharged 1200-horsepower Allison V12 driving its huge four-bladed prop, the P-51 didn't really take off until Britian's Royal Air Force officials in 1942 exchanged the Allison for their Spitfire

Some 25 years before Ford's Mustang arrived, North American Aviation was beginning production of this Mustang, the powerful P-51 fighter plane of World War II fame. This rare P-51D, owned by Henry "Butch" Schroeder of Danville, Illinois, is the F-6D photo reconnaissance derivative, a Mustang that carried both cameras and guns.

fighter's Rolls-Royce Merlin V12. Manufactured under license in this country by Packard, the superb supercharged 1400-hp Merlin transformed the Mustang from an average warplane into a dominating high-altitude hunter-killer. Top speed for the Merlin-powered P-51B was 440 mph, compared to 390 mph for the Allison-equipped P-51A. Additional modifications later upped the top-end ante to 487 mph for the P-51H.

Most plentiful among the various Mustang models was the P-51D, the first P-51 to use a modern-looking bubble canopy. Of some 8000 P-51Ds produced, 136 were modified to carry cameras as well as guns and redesignated for photo reconnaissance duty as F-6Ds. Owned by Henry "Butch" Schroeder of Danville, Illinois, the F-6D show here was painstakingly restored by Schroeder's ace righthand man, Mike Vadeboncouer, to represent "Lil' Margaret," the recon Mustang flown over Europe by Captain Clyde East. In typical fashion for a married fighter pilot, Captain East named his trusty mount after his wife.

Since, unlike most recon aircraft, camera-equipped Mustangs were heavily armed, F-6D pilots could ably "defend themselves," which Captain East did regularly. Flying for the 9th Air Force, 10th Photographic Reconnaissance Group, 15th Tactical Reconnaissance Squadron, Captain East scored 13 confirmed aerial kills, making him the leading American recon ace of the European theater. As for how well his Third Reich snapshots came out, no one quite recalls.

Whether supplying invaluable intelligence photography, defending B-17 bombers over Berlin, escorting B-29 Super Fortresses to Tokyo, strafing trains in Korea, or thrilling crowds as Reno air-racers, P-51

Mustangs have always soared high. It's little wonder John Najjar was impressed, so much so in 1962 he borrowed North American Aviation's Mustang moniker for Ford's two-seat, mid-engined ponycar "prototype."

The rest is history.

Lovingly restored, maintained and sometimes flown by Schroeder's ace mechanic Mike Vadeboncouer, this F-6D was modelled after the one flown by Captain Clyde East over Europe. As the markings on "Lil' Margaret" attest, East scored 13 air combat kills, making him the leading American recon ace.

4 1971-1973

More Mustang, Less Sales

If Lee Iacocca thought the '67 Mustang had been "a fat pig," it wouldn't have taken a rocket scientist to determine his opinion of Ford's all-new ponycar for 1971. All subjective responses to relative girth aside, the redesigned '71 Mustang was indeed a big automobile, much too big, in Iacocca's eyes, to be a ponycar. Practically everything about the machine was bigger compared to its 1970 predecessor. Wheelbase was up an inch while

The last great Boss Mustang was the Boss 351, a one-hit wonder for 1971. Like the Boss 302 small-block, the Boss 351's 351 HO V8 relied on Ford's excellent Cleveland heads with their canted valves and excellent breathing characteristics. Supporting cast included a Hurst-shifted four-speed, 3.91:1 Traction-Lok rearend, F60x15 rubber, competition suspension with staggered rear shocks, and power front discs.

total length grew two. Track was widened a whopping 3in in front, 2.5 in back, making room for a two-inch increase in body width. Up as well was curb weight, by about 250 pounds, and base price, a number that surpassed $3000 (for a V8 coupe) for the first time in Mustang history.

As in 1967, enlarging the Mustang in 1971 was basically a direct response to increasing competition in Detroit's hot-and-heavy horsepower race. Keeping up with the automaking Joneses in the late '60s meant producing more and more horses, which in turn meant bigger engines, which in turn meant bigger engine compartments and beefier platforms to handle all that power.

In 1970, Ford's all-new 429-cid 385-series V8—introduced for Thunderbirds in 1968—had superseded the aging FE-series V8 as the big-block performance leader in the company's full-sized ranks,

The 330hp 351 HO, for High Output, featured 11.7:1 compression, a solid-lifter cam and a 715-cfm four-barrel carburetor force fed through a ram-air hood. According to Motor Trend, *this combo beneath a '71 Boss 351 Mustang's hood was capable of 13.8-second blasts down the quarter-mile.*

leaving the vaunted 428 Cobra Jet FE to carry on for one last year as the Mustang's meat-and-potatoes muscle mill. With the newly expanded ponycar body on the scene in 1971, the bigger, better 429 CJ then replaced its 428 forerunner under that long, long hood, making for the largest, most powerful Mustang ever. Whether that result was good or bad is your call.

As for Iacocca, he of course wasn't pleased, and also wasn't shy about blaming one man for what he felt was the Mustang's wrong turn. Bunkie Knudsen, the former GM executive Henry Ford II had put ahead of Iacocca into Ford's president chair in February 1968, had needed only one look at chief designer Gary Halderman's mockup that same month to okay the basic design for the '71 Mustang. "We had never had approvals like that before," recalled Halderman, who himself wasn't all that excited about the Mustang's newfound mass. But two months after Bunkie's decision on the '71 model, the brawny 428 Cobra Jet debuted, and the Mustang was then off and running

Although the '71 Mach 1 was certainly sporty and definitely powerful, there was one negative aspect of the car most witnesses couldn't help but point out. Calling the '71 SportsRoof with its 14-degree "fastback" a "flat back," *Car Life's* critics explained that the car's "rear window would make a good skylight." "A glance in the rearview mirror," they continued, "provides an excellent view of the interior with a small band of road visible near the top of the mirror." And according to Sports Car Graphic, "the flat, minuscule rear backlite gives a beautiful view of the stars for two in the rear, but little else." In conclusion, however, Sports Car Graphic concluded that "whatever (the car) isn't, it is exciting, and... no Mach 1 is going to rust in a showroom."

towards its future as a high-powered heavyweight.

"Performance, performance, performance!" exclaimed Iacocca later, "that was what triggered [the Mustang] out of the small-car world. In 1968, in his autobiography, Knudsen added a monster engine with double the horsepower. To

The strongest Mustang powerplant in 1971 was the 385-series 429 Cobra Jet, superseding the FE-series 428 CJ of 1970. With or without optional ram-air equipment, the 429 CJ rated at 370 horsepower, enough oomph to propel a '71 Mach 1 through the lights at the far end of a quarter-mile in 13.97 seconds, according to Super Stock magazine.

support the engine, he had to widen the car. By 1971, the Mustang was no longer the same car, and declining sales figures were making the point clearly." Numbers didn't lie. Mustang sales dropped nearly 22 percent to 149,678 units for 1971, reflecting a descending trend that had continued steadily since 1966 as Detroit's ponycar pie was being sliced into smaller and smaller slabs.

The '72 Sprint convertible's patriotic interior featured vinyl bolstered seats with cloth inserts done in red, white and blue

If there was one consolation for Iacocca in 1971 it was that Bunkie wasn't around to revel in his handiwork. On September 11, 1969, only 18 months after he'd been hired, Knudsen was let go by Henry Ford II. Why the rapid firing? "I wish I could say Bunkie got fired because he ruined the Mustang or because his ideas were all wrong," wrote Iacocca. "But the actual reason was because he used to walk into Henry's office without knocking. That's right—without knocking!"

Certainly not sorry to see Knudsen go, Iacocca also recalled the event with a smile. "The day Bunkie was fired there was a great rejoicing and much drinking of champagne. Over in public relations, someone coined a phrase that became famous throughout the company: 'Henry Ford once said that history is bunk. But today, Bunkie is history.'" Fourteen

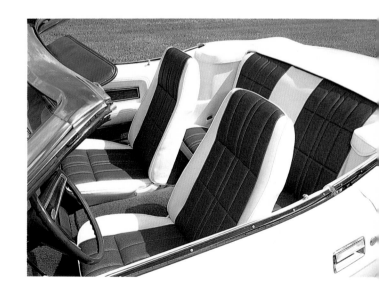

Based on the third of three Sprint packages offered over the years for the first-generation Mustang (following the 1966 and 1968 versions), the '72 "Olympic Sprint" convertible was a special package put together by the Washington D.C. area Ford dealers to commemorate both the 1972 Olympics and Washington's annual Cherry Blossom Parade.

Only 50 of these convertibles were built, all equipped identically, beginning with the optional Sprint package available on '72 hardtops and SportsRoofs. Special red/blue striping, a unique interior and "USA" shields on each rear quarter were the most noticeable Sprint features. All Sprint convertibles also had 302 V8s, AM/FM stereo and air conditioning.

Bottom: The last of the first-generation Mustangs, the 1973 model, differed little from its 1971 and '72 predecessors, especially when equipped with the optional exterior decor group, which, among other things, added a blacked-out grille and color-keyed bumper. Different grille arrangements helped set apart the base models in 1971, '72, and '73.

Right: The attractive forged-aluminum sport wheels were a new option for 1973. Additional extra-cost features on this '73 convertible include the Gold Glow metallic paint, black-accented "NASA" hood with ram-air, and trunk-mounted luggage rack.

months later, Iacocca became the top man in the Ford pecking order and immediately began promoting an idea first brought up as early as November 1969, a proposal to return the Mustang to its more polite, petite roots.

Iacocca's plan, however, wouldn't become reality until 1974. In the meantime, Bunkie's really big Mustang made its dealer debut in September 1970, then rolled on in similar fashion through three

Mustang convertible buyers in 1973 automatically received power front discs, knitted vinyl buckets, color-keyed carpeting, and a power top with backlite for their $3189 base price. Helping kick up the bottom line in a hurry here are air conditioning, AM/FM stereo, power steering, console, full instrumentation, and tinted glass.

model runs. Following the disappointing 22 percent sales drop for the new '71 model, Mustang production fell again in 1972, then rebounded slightly in 1973. By that time, high performance—Knudsen's inspiration for fattening up Iacocca's pony—had ironically all but faded away from the Detroit scene as tightened emissions restrictions, stricter safety standards, and sky-high insurance rates had put the brakes on the horsepower race.

Fading away as well were Ford's muscle Mustangs, cars like the formidable Boss 302 and Boss 429, both cancelled after 1970, leaving the Mach 1 to carry on as Dearborn's highest profile ponycar. The undeniably hot 429 Cobra Jet did remain a powerful option for one more year, then it too was cancelled after only 1,865 CJ Mach 1s were built for 1971. Top performance Mach 1s in 1972 and '73 relied on the 351 Cleveland small-block, a potent powerplant that nonetheless still fell short of the brutish big-block Cobra Jets as far as true tire-melting performance was concerned. At least in basic form. A beefed-up version of the 351 Cleveland small-block capable of doing battle with most big-blocks bullies did appear in 1971 to help remind the ponycar performance faithful that it is never really over until it's over.

Introduced in November 1970, the last of the great muscle Mustangs, the Boss 351, like the Mach 1, was offered only in SportsRoof form. Beneath its blacked-out, ram-air "NASA" hood was the 330-horse "351 HO" with its free-breathing, canted-valve Cleveland heads. Serious 351 HO features included a 715-cfm four-barrel, 11.7:1 compression, and a solid-lifter cam. Power front discs, a competition suspension with staggered rear shocks and F60x15 rubber, a Hurst-shifted four-speed, full instrumentation, twin twist locks on that black hood, a chin spoiler, and honeycomb grille completed the package, an impressive one to say the least.

According to *Car and Driver*, the Boss 351 offered "dragstrip performance that most cars with 100 cubic inches more displacement will envy." In a *Motor Trend* road test, a '71 Boss 351 scorched the quarter-mile in 13.8 seconds, results comparable to a '71 Mach 1 armed with a 429 Cobra Jet. That performance also ranked the Boss 351 right up among the hottest Fords ever. Nothing like going out with a bang. Although talk of a second-edition Boss 351 did make the rounds, the car ended up a one-hit wonder as the axe finally fell on Ford factory performance in 1972.

Innocent bystanders might've noticed the year before that something was up as the '70 Mach 1's base 351 was traded for a much more timid 302 Windsor standard small-block for the '71 Mach 1. Also indicative of changing times was the

An obvious sign that performance was no longer the going thing around Detroit, optional ram-air was only offered for the Mustang's 351 Cleveland 2V in 1973, leaving buyers of the more powerful 266hp four-barrel Cleveland small-block in a huff. Net output rating for this two-barrel 351, with or without ram-air, was 177 hp.

Mustang Grande's popularity rise. As performance dwindled, luxury became a more prominent ponycar selling point, with Grande sales jumping 28 percent in 1971. Two years later, the vinyl-roofed Grande hardtops made up nearly 20 percent—25,274 cars—of total Mustang production for 1973, the last year for Ford's first-generation pony.

5 1974-present

The Rest of the Ponycar Tale

It was. It is. Or at least so claims Ford's recent advertising campaign touting its all-new fourth-generation Mustang, an excellent upgrade of the long-hood/short-deck theme combining thoroughly modern engineering improvements with a retrofit essence of Iacocca's original ponycar flair. Replacing the long-running Fox chassis, first used way back in 1979, the redesigned SN-95 platform appeared in December 1993 sporting a

---

A convertible returned to the Mustang lineup in 1983 for the first time in 10 years while the GT's High Output (HO) 5.0L V8, in its second year, jumped up to 175 horsepower, thanks to the addition of a Holley four-barrel carburetor. Attractive aluminum wheels on the GT hatchback in back were part of the optional TRX suspension package. T-tops were also an option.

newfound firmer stance and wearing a restyled skin that left many Mustangers wondering why it took Dearborn so long to leave the aging third generation behind.

Of course, there were some who were sorry to see the Fox-chassis "Five-Oh" Mustang go, if only because it was the car responsible for replanting the Blue Oval performance banner smack-dab in the middle of the Camaro's roof during the mid-'80s. In doing so, Ford managed to pass Chevy's reigning champion in the "best bang for the bucks" derby, holding the lead firmly until the Bow-Tie boys unveiled their own all-new long-hood/short-deck creation late in 1992. Going on three years later, Mustang fans are still waiting to see whether or not Ford will retaliate soon with a more powerful ponycar, one better suited to run neck-and-neck with Chevy's 275hp LT1 Camaro. As they say, however, time alone will tell.

Lee Iacocca's "little jewel," the Mustang II, initially impressed everyone, including Motor Trend's *staff, who named it Car of the Year for 1974. But after sales skyrocketed to 385,993 for the first of the second-generation ponycars, the gleam quickly wore off this* really small gem, and not even a revival of the Cobra imagery or Mach 1 name could stem the tide. By 1979, it was time for a third-generation Mustang. This '75 Mustang II was one of 21,062 Mach 1 hatchbacks built that year.

Long respected for the way it could put a Camaro owner in his place, the Fox-chassis Mustang was also responsible for helping revive Ford's ponycar bloodline immediately following the Mustang II years of 1974-78. Both a response to purists' complaints concerning the "fattened-up" Mustangs of 1971-73 and an attempt to adapt to changing attitudes inspired by rising fuel prices, Iacocca's "little jewel" was initially well received as what Ford ads called "the right car at the right time." *Motor Trend's* editors apparently agreed wholeheartedly, bestowing the '74 Mustang II with their coveted "Car of the Year" award.

Created about the time disco was sweeping the land, Ford's '78 King Cobra was either the right car for the times or a really gaudy representation of just how off-the-wall the tape-and-stripe guys could get. Along with a large "Cobra" hood decal,

standard King Cobra features also included various striping, spoilers, and lower body spats. Suspension upgrades and eye-catching aluminum wheels were also part of the package. About 5000 were built.

In *Motor Trend's* words, the all-new second-generation ponycar was "a total departure from the fat old horse of the recent past... a rebirth of the Mustang of 1964-65—smaller and even more lithe in feel than the original pacesetter." Based on a Pinto platform and sporting sheet-metal originally designed by Italy's famed

Ghia design studio, the Mustang II measured 13 inches less hub-to-hub than its 1973 predecessor and was also four inches skinnier and roughly 300 pounds lighter. New engineering features included rack-and-pinion steering, improved noise and vibration reduction, and a penny-pinching 2.3-liter four-cylinder engine standard. No V8 was initially offered, only an optional 2.8-liter V6.

Yet even without any real performance appeal, the '74 Mustang II brought buyers running into Ford dealerships. At least at first. Mustang sales nearly tripled for 1974, hitting 385,993, reminding some of the mad rush of April 1964. Then came

lowing year did little to stem the tide as customers grew less enchanted with the Mustang II's cramped quarters and weak performance. Although sales did rise nearly 25 percent for 1978, by then the deal was already done, and not even the high-profile King Cobra, with its flashy decals and snazzy spats and spoilers,

In 1964, Ford's first Mustang was honored by its selection to pace the Indianapolis 500. Fifteen years later, the first third-generation ponycar received the same honor, only this time Dearborn took advantage of the situation and marketed about 11,000 Indy Pace Car replicas. Both 302 V8 and turbocharged four-cylinder versions were built.

rapid decline. A 51 percent drop in sales for 1975 was followed by a steady slide in 1976 and '77. Introduction of a lukewarm, optional 302 V8 in 1975 and the token revival of the Cobra name—appearing as the taped-and-striped Cobra II—the fol-

could save the day for the second-generation Mustang.

Commonly taken out of context, the Mustang II is an easy target today for probably too many slings and arrows. But in all fairness, even those among the ponycar crowd who still have a soft spot in their hearts for the little Mustang II have to admit it was one of Ford's better ideas that deserved to run its course. Quickly.

So it was that big plans for yet another all-new Mustang were in the works even as the first Mustang IIs were rolling off the

ary 1973. Dearborn's first Fox-chassis cars, Ford's Fairmont and Mercury's Zephyr, debuted in August 1977, followed by a Mustang/Capri version a year later.

Seemingly defying physical laws, the '79 "Fox" Mustang was wider, longer and taller than the Mustang II, yet was 200 pounds lighter. Jack Telnack's styling team

Ford celebrated 20 years of ponycar history with a special '84-1/2 anniversary model, available as a hatchback or convertible. All 20th anniversary cars were painted Oxford White with "GT 350" identification. Power

came from either a 5.0L V8 or the 2.3L turbo four. This V8 20th anniversary Mustang was one of 3,900 hatchbacks sold; another 5,260 convertibles were also produced.

trucks in rapid fashion. In December 1974, Iacocca and Henry Ford II gave two thumbs up to the Fox project, a design for a pair of fuel-efficient model lines first seen in official Ford paperwork in Febru-

did the attractive shell, which rolled on a new chassis featuring MacPherson struts up front and a coil-spring, four-link suspension in back. Again, a 2.3-liter four-cylinder was standard, but optional under-

hood fare included a turbocharged four and a 130hp 5.0-liter (302 cid) V8. Signs perhaps that performance and prestige would again become Ford Mustang's middle name? Yes, according to *Motor Trend's* John Ethridge, who claimed the third-generation pony could "now compete both in the marketplace and on the road with lots of cars that used to outclass it."

As in 1974, Mustang sales again soared, jumping some 92 percent in 1979 to 369,936 cars. And as in 1964, the new Mustang was chosen to pace the Indianapolis 500. About 11,000 regular-production Indy Pace Car replicas were built with both 5.0L and turbo four power. Included in the deal were special graphics and the sport-minded TRX suspension.

Suitably honored and definitely hot to trot, the Fox-chassis Mustang then set out on a steady uphill climb towards Detroit's low-priced performance pinnacle. First came the 157hp High-Output (HO) 5.0L two-barrel in 1982, the year the

Initially rated at 175 horsepower, the SVO 2.3-liter intercooled turbocharged four-cylinder jumped to 205 horses in 1985, then dropped back to 200 horsepower for the car's final year in 1986.

Left: Introduced in 1984, Ford's SVO (Special Vehicle Operations) Mustang returned as '85, '85-1/2 and '86 models. All were easily identified by their assymetrical hood scoops, aero noses, and multi-level rear spoilers, but the most intriguing aspects of the SVO involved its turbo-four power source and its hot-handling suspension. In all, 9,844 were built, including 3,314 '86 models, like this one, for domestic sales.

Mustang GT returned after a 12-year hiatus. In 1983, a Holley four-barrel went atop the 175hp 5.0L HO and a convertible rejoined the ponycar lineup for the first time since 1973.

Big news for 1984 involved the debut of the Euro-style SVO Mustang, initially powered by a 175hp intercooled 2.3-liter turbo four. Featuring Koni gas-charged shocks, four-wheel discs, 16-inch wheels, and a Hurst-shifted five-speed, the SVO Mustang hit 205 horsepower in 1985, then was detuned down to 200 in its final form for 1986. In all, 9,844 were built during the three-year SVO run.

Aero styling up front was added in 1987, as were 15-inch "turbine" wheels for the GT. Essentially unchanged, the same package carried over into the following year, as this '88 GT convertible attests. Restyled 16-inch GT wheels were added in 1991.

As for additional basic upgrades, quad shocks were added in back for 1984, just in time to help celebrate the Mustang's 20th birthday. Offered as a hatchback and convertible with either 2.3-liter turbo four or 5.0 V8 power, the limited-edition '84-1/2 20th Anniversary models featured Oxford White paint with red "G.T. 350" lower body-side stripes.

In 1985, tubular headers with dual exhausts (from the catalytic converters back) and roller lifters boosted HO output to 210 horsepower, the most for a carbureted 5.0 small-block. True dual exhausts were added the following year, when the 5.0's four-barrel carb was exchanged for the EEC (electronic energy control) EFI (electronic fuel injection) equipment. By 1987, the EFI 5.0 HO was putting out 225 horses, enough to propel the revised "aero-look" Mustang

Few could beat the Mustang's electronic fuel-injected (EFI) 5.0L HO in 1988. With a roller cam and tubular exhaust headers, the 5.0 HO put out 225 real horses, power enough to make the lightweight LX coupe a low-14-second screamer in the quarter-mile. Camaro owners never had a chance.

through the quarter-mile in a tad more than 14 seconds. Camaro drivers didn't stand a chance, and growing popularity of the hot 5.0 Mustang—either in GT or lighter LX form—helped convince Dearborn to give up ill-advised plans to replace the Fox-chassis Mustang with a Mazda-based front-driver, a platform that instead appeared as the '89 Probe.

Recognizing a winner, designers then basically left the Fox chassis well enough alone, with one of the most noticeable changes being larger, restyled 16-inch GT wheels, added in 1991. Ford did, howev-

A revised, greatly stiffened chassis and four-wheel disc brakes made the all-new '94 Mustang a much more firm, sure-footed ride compared to its Fox chassis predecessors.

And while GTs were all powered by the ever-present 5.0L V8, base models dumped their standard four-cylinders in favor of a 145hp 3.8L V6.

Although it was downrated to 215 horsepower, the '94 Mustang GT's 5.0L HO small-block is still a free-wheeling, fun machine. Notice the new brace added between the cowl and upper shock towers, one of the many engineering additions made to make the '94 Mustang platform more rigid.

er, save the best for last in 1993 as the Special Vehicle Team rolled out its 235hp Cobra, a certified throwback to the street racers Carroll Shelby once built. Even more reminiscent of Shelby's handiwork was SVT's R-model '93 Cobra, which, like Shelby American's GT 350R of 1965, meant business. As if you couldn't have guessed, "R" still stands for "racing."

And the Mustang still stands for fun, even after three decades on the road. "It is what it was, and more," announced ads for Ford's all-new fourth-generation

ponycar. Who's to argue? Consider the '94 Mustang's standard four-wheel discs and its improved chassis/body design that did away with the NVH (noise, vibration, harshness) problems inherent with the Fox chassis; throw in superior handling and a new base 3.8L V6 instead of a standard four-cylinder, and there your have it—the best Mustang yet.

Can it get any better? Ask again in another 30 years.

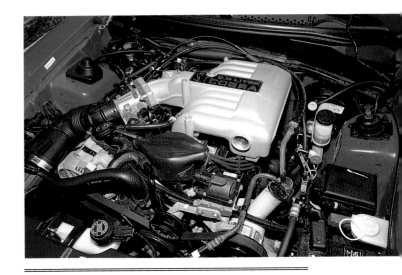

Venom for the '94 Cobra came from a pumped-up version of the GT's 215hp 5.0L small-block. A more aggressive cam, GT40 cast-iron heads, revised intake gear and less restrictive exhausts let loose an additional 25 more horses for the Cobra. Unfortunately, installing the larger induction setup meant losing the new Mustang's shock-tower-to-cowl brace, a piece that helped stiffen the latest ponycar platform.

Left: Differences setting a '94 SVT Cobra Mustang apart from its GT cousin include clear-lens headlights, special front fascia with round foglamps, chromed 17x8 wheels (with dark accents on Indy Pace Car convertibles—wheels on Cobra coupes are fully chromed), appropriate yet nearly unnoticable coiled-snake fender emblems, and a unique rear spoiler. Only 1000 Indy Pace Car replicas, all Rio Red '94 Cobra convertibles with saddle interiors and tan tops, were built by Ford's Special Vehicle Team. SVT also rolled out 5,009 '94 Cobra coupes in red, black and white.

6 Variations On A Theme

Ponycar Spin-Offs from Shelby to Saleen

Ford's popular ponycar has meant various things to various people during its three decades on this planet. Budget buggy with a sporty flair. Road-hugging street racer. Tire-melting Saturday night warrior. Semi-plush bou-

Not all Mustang variants were meant for the streets. While Carroll Shelby was busy in California building his GT 350 road warriors, the speed kings at Holman-Moody in Charlotte, North Carolina, were working on a red-hot Mustang of their own. Holman-Moody's product was an altered-wheelbase drag car intended for Factory Experimental (FX) competition. This '65 A/FX Mustang, one of 15 built by Holman-Moody, was originally modified for Larson Ford in White Plains, New York. It is also one of seven equipped with Ford's outrageous SOHC 427 V8. The other eight were originally powered by 427 "High-Riser" wedge-head V8s.

levard cruiser. The Mustang has worn all these hats and more, thanks both to the Better Idea guys in Dearborn and a few independent thinkers outside the company.

Some of these outsiders, like the legendary Carroll Shelby and Steve Saleen on the West Coast are certainly well known. Others, like Dario Orlando in Florida, are less so, but their creations speak for themselves, loud and clear. Specialty Mustangs, from Shelby's first fire-breathing GT 350 in 1965 to Saleen's latest low-slung S-351, stand as just as much a prominent part of Ford's ponycar history as the regular-production models and rightly so since Dearborn has been more than willing to "support" these various projects one way or the other over the years.

Shelby, of course, kicked things off in the specialty Mustang market not long

With an overhead cam in each head and hemispherical combustion chambers, the 427 SOHC, or "Cammer" as it was known, could wind out like no other big-block out there. Output was in the 600 horsepower neighborhood. Although various rumors beginning in 1964 spoke of a regular-production Cammer, no 427 SOHC V8s ever made it to the street in a standard-issue Ford.

after Iacocca's first pony hit the road some 30 years ago. At the time, the famed Texas-chicken-rancher-turned-race-driver was two years into production of his little Anglo-American hybrid racer, the AC Cobra, a British sports car shell powered by a warmed-over Blue-Oval small-block V8. Dearborn officials, however, preferred to see a more recognizable Ford product taking checkered

flags, and what better candidate for that job than the new Mustang? A deal was then made to supply the Shelby American plant in Venice, California, with bare-bones Mustang fastbacks and Shelby's crew did the rest, with production of the race-ready GT 350 beginning in October 1964, followed by the official public unveiling January 27, 1965.

"Pretty much a brute of a car," according to *Road & Track*, the '65 GT 350 was meant for one thing, and a night on the town wasn't it. As Shelby later told *Sports Cars of the World* magazine in 1971, "my idea was to build a car that would outrun the Corvette and Ferrari production cars." Winning Sports Car Club of America (SCCA) B/Production races was the goal, and Shelby's GT 350 didn't disappoint.

"The thing was a racing car in disguise and not much of a disguise at that," recalled *Car Life's* Joe Scalzo in 1969. There were no ifs, ands, or buts about the first GT 350 and no nonsense, either. No backseat, no automatic transmission, no color choices—all '65 GT 350s had black interiors and white exteriors with optional Guardsman Blue "LeMans" stripes available. Beneath that pale skin was a bone-jarring suspension featuring lowered upper A-arms and special underhood bracing up front, over-ride torque control arms in back, and Koni adjustable shocks all around. A bullet-proof racheting Detroit Locker rearend was standard, as were the loud cutout exhaust pipes exiting directly in front of each rear tire.

Power for the beast came from a modified Hi-Po 289 fed by a 715-cfm Holley four-barrel on an aluminum intake. An enlarged aluminum oil pan, special "Tri-Y" headers and twin glass-

machine that, in the opinion of *Car Life's* Jim Wright, was what "most of us wanted the original Mustang to be in the first place." Shelby American built 562 GT 350s for 1965, including 37 truly serious R-model all-out racers.

Although Shelby American tried the trick again in 1966, pressures from Dear-

Per Ford's instructions, Shelby American toned down its GT 350 image in 1966, adding full exhaust pipes, a backseat, an optional automatic transmission and multiple paint choices. Rear quarter glass and bodyside scoops were also added.

pack mufflers were also part of the deal, which added up to 306 horsepower. Throw in a scooped fiberglass hood, a four-speed, 9.5-inch front discs, and heavy-duty 15-inch station wagon wheels, and you were ready to race in a

born to tone down the GT 350's roughness left Carroll Shelby with a bad taste in his mouth. Ford wanted a wider market for the car, with the obvious goal being to sell more Shelby Mustangs to drivers who didn't necessarily want to go racing.

Although changes were made outside and underneath, the GT 350 power source in 1966 was still the "Shelby-ized" High Performance 289, rated at 306 horsepower in Shelby trim.

Shelby updates in 1967 included various fiberglass add-ons up front and at the tail and a new model, the big-block GT 500, powered by a 355hp 428. This '67 GT 500 has the optional Le Mans stripes.

Previously standard, the Koni shocks and Detroit Locker went to the options list, the rear torque arms were replaced by simpler underslung traction bars, and the lowered front suspension was discontinued to cut costs. Full dual exhausts went underneath, a backseat went inside, and an optional C4 automatic joined the standard Borg-Warner T-10 four-speed. Five paint choices were also added, as were functional bodyside side scoops and distinctive rear quarter

Shelby GT 350 and GT 500 production was transferred from the Shelby American works in California to the A.O. Smith facility near Detroit in 1968. Then in 1969, an even more stylized Shelby Mustang appeared featuring a radically redesigned nose. Tail features remained similar to the '67-68 look with its sequential turn signal taillights and ducktail spoiler. Center-mounted exhaust tips were new for 1969. Standard power for this Black Jade '69 GT 350 was a 351 Windsor V8.

glass. Clearly more socially acceptable, the '66 GT 350 attracted nearly 2400 buyers, including the Hertz Rent-A-Car company, which put 1000 Shelbys into its fleet in 1966.

Despite the sales success, Shelby never did like the direction his specialty Mustangs took after 1965. Today, his favorite is still that first GT 350, "a no compromise car [that was] built to get the job done."

But that changed once Ford began taking more interest in the project in 1966. "All of the corporate vultures jumped on the thing and that's when it started going to hell," recalled Shelby in 1971. "I started trying to get out of the deal in 1967, and it took me until 1970 to get production shut down."

Of course, Shelby's standards were much higher than the typical enthusiast,

Regardless of what engine was under the hood, Shelby Mustang interiors were always sporty and purposeful. Notice the shoulder harnesses inside this '69 GT 350.

Convertible Shelby Mustangs first appeared in 1968, the same year the GT 500KR—"KR" for "King of the Road"—debuted. Heart of the KR was the new 335hp 428 Cobra Jet V8.

The KR designation was dropped in 1969 as all GT 500s were Cobra Jets, as is this big-block Shelby convertible, one of 335 built during the 1969-70 run.

who continued buying Shelby Mustangs even as the car's creator was trying to put on the brakes. Sure, Shelbys to follow may not have been as mean as the '65, but they did have their own appeal, both from an image perspective and as real performers.

Shelby news for 1967 included revised styling and a new model, the big-block-powered GT 500. An extended fiberglass snout and Kamm-back tail improved Shelby Mustang looks considerably in 1967, and an

even more distinctive facade was created in 1969 once Ford stylists took complete control. Following the 1967 remake, Shelby Mustang production were transferred from Shelby's Los Angeles plant to the A.O. Smith company in Livonia, Michigan, where the renamed "Shelby Cobra GT 350/500" was built up through 1970.

A convertible Shelby appeared in 1968, as did the midyear GT 500KR, "KR" standing for "King of the Road." Heart of the GT 500KR was the 335hp

With the project all but winding down, Shelby production for 1970 basically involved repackaging 1969 leftovers. "Repackaging" meant adding black stripes to the hood and a chin spoiler below the nose. This '70

GT 500 is powered by a 428 Super Cobra Jet, an engine created by adding the Drag Pack option, which among other things included an easily identifiable engine oil cooler in front of the radiator.

428 Cobra Jet, a musclebound big-block that revived memories of the bully the Shelby Mustang had once been. By 1969, however, the end of the trail was in sight, and only remarketing leftovers into 1970 kept the Shelby Mustang alive for one last fling.

Fourteen years later, SCCA racer Steve Saleen picked up the ball and joined the specialty Mustang game, forming Saleen Autosport in Petulma, California. Initially, the Saleen Mustang's main attraction was its "Racecraft Suspension" package, which lowered

Like the almost-forgotten Mustang I racer of 1962, the ASC/McLaren Mustang convertibles built between 1987 and 1990 were all two-seaters. One of a mere 65 built for 1990, this ASC/McLaren Mustang is the only one featuring a silver exterior and maroon top and interior. Although the folding tops on these cars were manual, they were easily stowed, even by one person.

the car about 1.5 inches and added, among other things, Bilstein shocks and struts and Goodyear Eagle rubber on 15x7 Hayashi alloy wheels. Sure, the '84 Saleen Mustang was also a real looker with its distinctive striping and functional airdam, spoilers, and skirts, but it was the car's superb track-ready handling that made its $14,300 sticker seem a steal.

Up through 1993, Saleen Autosport had delivered more than 2600 of its hot-handling horses, all sporting that unmistakable Saleen rear spoiler. Advancements over the years included adding 16-inch wheels in 1986, an upper shock tower brace and four-wheel disc brakes in 1987, and a new model in 1989 to help celebrate the Mustang's 25th birthday.

Not an official 25th anniversary Mustang, the '89 Saleen SSC was nonetheless a celebration in itself, with a specially modified 300hp 5.0L beneath its hood and a whole host of heavy-duty hardware throughout. Included as well, of course, were the proven Racecraft parts, high-profile Saleen body add-ons, and various special SSC graphics and interior appointments. Priced at $36,500, the limited-edition '89 SSC hatchback attracted only 160 buyers. Even more limited was the equally impressive 304hp Saleen SC introduced in 1990. A mere 11 were built

Although cash-flow difficulties have severely limited total Saleen production after 1990, the intriguing breed has managed to survive. And with the arrival of the fourth-generation Mustang came Steve Saleen's latest project, the S-351, with its 351 Windsor small-block, an engine that reportedly dynoes at around 370 horses. Whatever the '65 Shelby "was," this latest specialty Mustang "is" in spades. Zero to 60 in 5.9 seconds, a quarter-mile pass in 8.4 ticks more, a top speed of, say, 170 mph, and 0.97g on the skidpad, all for $33,500. Does it get any better?

Dario Orlando thinks so. Orlando's Steeda Autosports, in Pompano Beach, Florida, is one of the newest kids on the specialty Mustang block, having been in the business for some seven years now. Although Orlando prefers to concentrate on the sales of Motorsport parts and various exclusive Steeda hop-up kits for five-liter Mustangs, his shop had converted, between 1988 and '93, about 400 Fox-chassis Five-Ohs into some of the best handling, hottest-running, quickest braking ponycars on the road. And they didn't stop there.

Like Saleen, Steeda Autosports has also jumped on the all-new Mustang bandwagon for 1994, introducing easily the best Steeda Mustang yet. For about $7000 above a base '94 Mustang sticker—$17,300 for the coupe, $22,000 convertible—Steeda adds its proven G-Trac sport suspension, which includes lowered, stiffer springs, urethane bushings and cross-bracing up front, an additional sway bar (joining the stock unit) in back, and 17-inch wheels at the corners. Standard Mustang four-wheel discs are upgraded with Steeda's own high-perfor-

Known for their excellent Racecraft Suspension, Saleen Mustangs also stand out in a crowd thanks to their large rear spoilers, 16-inch American Racing basketweave wheels (in this case), and noticeably lowered stance. Reportedly, 105 black Saleens like this one were built in 1987, with total production for all colors reaching 278.

mance carbon-metallic pads, and power comes from a 290hp 5.0L with GT40 heads and intake. Orlando plans to build 100 of these '94 super 'Stangs. Not as noticeable on the street as a Saleen, a Steeda Mustang nonetheless can give its West Coast counterpart all it can handle.

In between the time Saleen set up shop in California and Steeda got rolling in Florida, two Livonia, Michigan, firms joined forces to create another specialty Mustang, this one concentrating more on prestige. Engine builder Bruce McLaren and the American Sunroof Company first teamed up in Livonia late in 1983, working together to produce the ASC/McLaren Capri, a distinctive Fox-chassis machine offered up through 1986 in coupe and convertible form. Founded in 1965 by West German engineer Heinz Prechter, ASC has since grown into the world's leading OEM convertible conversion company, having produced more than 400,000 droptop models for 12 different manufacturers, foreign and domestic. Today, 25 percent of convertibles sold worldwide are ASC products.

In 1987, ASC/McLaren shifted its focus to Ford Motor Company's other Fox platform, introducing an attractive two-seat Mustang roadster that showed off ASC's convertible conversion expertise. The process began with a specially prepared LX "notchback" coupe supplied off Ford's assembly line with convertible cowl support and chassis bracing. After delivery to ASC, the LX Mustang's top was sheared off, the windshield frame was bent back some 10 degrees, more reinforcement was added, and a special "tub" was dropped into the abandoned rear seat area as a housing for the folding Cambria soft top. A rear-hinged steel deck then went on to cover the top storage area. GT lower body cladding, a leather-wrapped steering wheel and shift knob, unique wheels, special taillight covers, and a new rear fascia completed the package. Options included Recaro leather seats and all other typical extra-cost Mustang features.

Production of ASC/McLaren Mustang convertibles was 479 in 1987, 1000 in 1988, 247 in 1989, and 65 in 1990, the last year for the unique two-seater, a car that proved that specialty Mustangs could be classy, too.

Whoever said variety is the spice of life must have been a Mustang owner.

Southern Californian Steve Saleen's counterpart across the country is Dario Orlando, of Steeda Autosports in Pompano Beach, Florida. Orlando's Steeda Mustangs also rely on a superb suspension, the "G-trac"

system, and in the case of this '94 model, are powered by a 290hp derivative of the GT's 215hp 5.0L HO small-block. Various options and performance packages can tailor a Steeda Mustang to the individual driver's tastes.

Index